Conures as Pets

Including Information about Sun Conures and Green-Cheeked Conures

Care, training, breeding, diet, lifespan, sounds, behavior, health, mutations, where to buy, and Green Cheeked Parakeet and Sun Parakeet comparison

By Taylor David

Conures as Pets

Including Information about Sun Conures and Green-Cheeked Conures

Care, training, breeding, diet, lifespan, sounds, behavior, health, mutations, where to buy, and Green Cheeked Parakeet and Sun Parakeet comparison

ISBN: 978-1-927870-23-5

Copyright © 2013 by Ubiquitous Publishing
First Edition, 2013
ubiquitouspublishing.com

Author: Taylor David
Published by: Ubiquitous Publishing

Published in Canada
Printed in the USA

Conures as Pets

A Complete Owner's Guide

Including Information about Sun Conures and
Green-Cheeked Conures

Acknowledgements

My sincerest thanks to my loving family and supportive friends for their help in making this book a reality. I would never have been able to finish without the patient encouragement of my family and the thorough proofreading and critiques of my closest friends.

Table of Contents

Chapter One: Introduction

If you have ever stopped into your local pet store and been caught by the sight of a bright green or yellow bird, you may have been looking at a Conure. Conures are parrots belonging to several genera and species but the most popular species for pets are Green-Cheeked and Sun Conures. These birds are known for their brilliant colors and loved for their social and affectionate personalities.

In this book you will learn everything there is to know about keeping Conures as pets. Starting with general information about these beautiful birds and ending with common mistakes, this book is a comprehensive resource on Green-Cheeked and Sun Conures. If you are thinking about buying a Conure as a pet, take the time to learn as much as you can about these birds first. The more you know, the more equipped you will be to provide your Conures with the best care possible.

Chapter Two: Understanding Conures

The most important thing to realize about Conures is that the name "conure" applies to a group of parrots, not a particular species. Think of it this way – all Conures are parrots, but not all parrots are Conures. In this chapter you will learn the basics about Conures as a group as well as more detailed information about two of the most popular species. The information you learn in this chapter will prepare you for the tips and advice in the rest of the book.

1.) What Are Conures?

The term "conure" is loosely applied to a group of small to medium-sized parrots belonging to the New World subfamily of parrots. These birds belong to several genera of birds including small parrots and large parakeets. Similar in size and lifestyle to Australian parakeets and Old World rose-ringed parakeets, Conures typically live in Central and South America.

As a group, Conures are known for their attention-seeking behavior. In fact, they have been nicknamed the "clowns" of the parrot world, often seen hanging upside down or swaying from branches. These birds have long tails with a light build and small, strong beaks. In most species, the beak of a Conure is black or horn-colored with a small cere – a waxy structure that covers the base of the beak, sometimes feathered.

In the wild, Conures tend to live in flocks of 20 or more birds of the same species. These birds subsist on grain and, as such, are regarded as agricultural pests in some areas. Because there are several species identified as Conures, it is impossible to create a general description to fit Conures as a whole. The main genera classified under the term "Conure" include the genera *Aratinga* and *Pyrrhura*. Most of the other genera classified as Conures contain only one or two species.

Perhaps the two most popular species of Conure are the Green-Cheeked Conure and the Sun Conure. Both of these species are popular as pets and come in a variety of colors. There are six subspecies of Green-Cheeked Conure (genus *Pyrrhura*) but only one type of Sun Conure (genus *Aratinga*). You will learn more about both of these species in detail in the next section.

2.) Facts about Conures

As you've already learned, it is difficult to list facts about Conures in general because the term "conure" is used to classify a rather large grouping of birds. In this section you will receive basic facts about the two most popular types of Conures kept as pets – Green-Cheeked Conures and Sun Conures. These facts may help you to decide if, in fact, a Conure is the right pet for you and, if so, which species.

a.) Green-Cheeked Conures

The Green-Cheeked Conure is also called the green-cheeked parakeet and it is a member of the genus Pyrrhura of the subfamily Arinae. The species name of this bird is *Pyrrhura molinae*, or *P. molinae* for short. There are six subspecies of Green-Cheeked Conure including: *P.m. australis*, *P.m. flavoptera*, *P.m. hypoxantha*, *P.m. molinae*, *P.m. phoenicura* and *P.m. restricta*.

Generally, Green-Cheeked Conures measure about 10 inches (26 cm) long and weigh between 2.0 and 2.8 ounces (60 to 80 g). As suggested by the name, these parrots have green feathers on the body and cheeks with a brown, black or grey crown. The primary wing feathers are blue, the tailmaroon and the beak grey. In some specimens, these birds have short transverse striations on the breast and red coloration on the abdomen. In terms of appearance, both males and females of the species exhibit the same coloration.

Green-Cheeked Conures can be found through southern and west-central Brazil and throughout northern and eastern Bolivia. They have also been found in parts of Paraguay and Argentina. The primary habitat of these birds is forest and woodland where they can be found in flocks of 10 to 20 individuals. These flocks spend most of their time at treetop level and, when food is abundant, the flocks can grow much larger than previously stated.

These birds have started to become incredibly popular as pets for a number of reasons. Though still fairly loud (as most birds are), Green-Cheeked Conures do tend to be quieter than most species of parakeet. This species can also be trained to perform simple tricks and to speak with a very limited vocabulary if provided extensive training.

What makes these birds wonderful companion pets is the fact that they are playful and affectionate. Green-Cheeked Conures have been labeled for having a "big personality in a small body." Unlike some birds, these parrots enjoy being held, though they are prone to biting while still young. These birds enjoy a diet of seeds and grains supplemented with fresh fruits and commercial pellets.

In addition to their natural coloration, there are four different color mutations which have been selectively bred in Green-Cheeked Conures. These mutations include: cinnamon, pineapple, turquoise and yellow-sided. Cinnamon variants have a pale, lime-green coloration to the feathers with a tan head. The tail feathers in this mutation are a lighter purple than the typical Green-Cheeked Conure.

Green-Cheeked Conure, Pineapple Mutation

In pineapple mutations, the breast is brightly colored with a tan head and lime-green feathers on the back. Turquoise mutations have a blue-green tint to the feathers on their bodies and the breast and tail feathers are grey. Yellow-sided mutations exhibit a brightly colored chest of yellow and orange feathers. Another mutation of green/red/blue apple is possible as well but not very common.

b.) Sun Conures

Also called Sun Parakeets, Sun Conures are a medium-sized parrot native to the northeastern portion of South America. These birds are known for their bright colors, having predominantly golden feathers with and orange face and underparts. The golden coloration is least diluted on the upper portion of the wings which are tipped in green and the orange coloration is most heavily concentrated around the eyes. The tail is typically olive-green with a blue tip while the flight feathers are dark grey.

Sun Conures are often confused with Sulphur-Breasted Parakeets and Jandaya Parakeets due to their similar appearance. Jandaya Parakeets, however, have entirely green wings while Sulphur-Breasted Parakeets have green mottling and less orange coloration. Male and female Sun

Conures are nearly identical in appearance, though juveniles of the species exhibit more green coloration than mature adults.

The taxonomy of the Sun Conure dates all the way back to the 18th century when Linnaeus originally described the species in his *Systema Naturae*. These birds were originally classified in the genus *Psittacus* but have since been transferred to *Aratinga* along with several other New World species of parrot. The Sun Conure is monotypic which means that there are no associated subspecies.

Sun Conure

Unfortunately, the Sun Conure is an endangered species –
its population is threatened by loss of habitat and over-
trapping for the pet trade. These beautiful birds are not as
well understood as Green-Cheeked Conures because they
are difficult to study in the wild. Though once listed as
"Least Concern" by IUCN surveys, a recent survey
conducted in Guyana resulted in an uplisting to
Endangered in 2008. Though regularly bred in captivity, the
population of this species in the wild has dwindled
dangerously and continues to remain unstable.

As pets, Sun Conures are popular for their brilliant
coloration. Compared to other species, however, they can
be very loud and often have an inquisitive temperament.
This being the case, Sun Conures often need a great deal of
attention and they are prone to making a lot of noise if they
do not get it. Though still able to achieve a limited
vocabulary through extensive training, the Sun Conure
doesn't adapt as well to speech as the Green-Cheeked
Conure. These birds are also heavy chewers so they need
plenty of toys and treats to keep them occupied.Because
they can be fairly loud, Sun Conures may not be ideal for
small apartments where noise may bother neighbors.

c.) Summary of Facts

Classification: subfamily Arinae, tribe Arini

Species Name: *Pyrrhura molinae* (Green-Cheeked Conure); *Aratinga solstitialis* (Sun Conure)

Distribution: South America

Habitat (Green-Cheeked Conure): primarily forest and woodland; typically found at treetop level

Habitat (Sun Conure): savanna, coastal forests, foothills

Social Groups: typically flocks of 10 to 20, up to 30

Size: 10 inches (26 cm) Green-Cheeked Conure; 12 inches (30 cm) Sun Conure

Weight: 2.0 to 2.8 oz. (60 to 80 g) Green-Cheeked Conure; 4 oz. (110 g) Sun Conure

Primary Coloration: green body, blue wings, maroon tail (Green-Cheeked Conure); yellow body, orange chest and head, green tail and wing tips (Sun Conure)

Diet: nuts, seeds, berries and fruit

Noise Level: moderate (Green-Cheeked); very loud (Sun)

Training: can be taught limited vocabulary, can imitate humans to some degree, may be taught simple tricks

Temperament (Green-Cheeked Conure): playful and affectionate, enjoys being held

Temperament (Sun Conure): can be inquisitive, demands a great deal of attention

Lifespan: 15 to 30 years

3.) Natural History of Green-Cheeked Conures

Even though the Green-Cheeked Conure is very popular in the pet industry, it has not been widely studied in the wild. One of the most comprehensive studies on the species was conducted in 2007 and published in the *Brazilian Journal of Biology*. In 2004, the first IUCN survey of the species identified it as a species of Least Concern. The same assessment was made in 2008, 2009 and, most recently, in 2012. Despite the "Least Concern" assessment of the species, numbers of Green-Cheeked Conure have significantly declined in the wild due to habitat destruction and trapping for the pet trade.

Unfortunately, the history of the Sun Conure is a different story. The first assessment of the species was taken in 1988 when the Sun Conure was listed as "Near Threatened". By the time of the next survey in 2004, the population had increased and the species was given a label of "Least Concern." Four years later, however, the population had declined to the point of endangerment and, as of 2012, it continues to decline. Once common throughout Guyana and Brazil, the Sun Conure has been extirpated since the 1970s and is currently scarce or completely absent in much of its former range.

4.) *Types of Conures*

As you already know, there are six different subspecies of Green-Cheeked Conure but Sun Conures are monotypic. The six subspecies of Green-Cheeked Conure include:

Pyrrhura molinaeaustralis

Pyrrhura molinaeflavoptera

Pyrrhura molinaehypoxantha

Pyrrhura molinae molinae

Pyrrhura molinaephoenicura

Pyrrhura molinaerestricta

There is little to distinguish the subspecies from the main species except for color variation and distribution. Little information regarding these differences is available aside from the fact that *Pyrrhura molinaehypoxantha*was originally classified as *Pyrrhura molinae sordida*. This subspecies occurs naturally as a green or yellow color morph of the Green-Cheeked Conure.

a.) Natural Range of Green-Cheeked Conure Subspecies:

Pyrrhura molinaeaustralis

Southern Bolivia and northwestern Argentina

Pyrrhura molinaeflavoptera

Cochabamba on the La Paz border in northern Bolivia

Pyrrhura molinaehypoxantha

Southern Brazil and northwestern Paraguay

Pyrrhura molinae molinae

Highlands of eastern Bolivia

Pyrrhura molinaephoenicura

Southern Brazil and northeastern Bolivia

Pyrrhura molinaerestricta

Santa Cruz in eastern Bolivia

Chapter Three: What to Know Before You Buy

Because Conures can live 15 to 25 years or longer, buying one as a pet is a long-term commitment. Before you buy a Conure, take the time to make sure you can provide the care your bird deserves. In this chapter, you will learn about the licensing requirements to keep Conures as pets along with some basic info including whether Conures can be kept with other pets and the costs you can expect in buying and keeping a Conure.

1.) Do You Need a License?

When it comes to the laws regarding keeping Conures as pets, there are a few things you need to think about. The first thing to think about is whether or not they are legal in your area at all – some states and municipalities have strict regulations regarding the types of animals you can keep as pets. Not only do you need to think about whether it is legal to keep Conures in your area, but you also have to think about whether you need a special permit to import, export or breed them – you should also consider whether there is a legal limit to the number of Conures you can keep.

a.) Licensing in the U.S.

In the United States, there are many laws regarding the import, export and keeping of wild or exotic animals. Domestic animals like cats and dogs are subject to less rigorous regulation, but a permit may still be required to keep them. Before you go out and buy a Conure, you would be wise to find out whether there are any zoning laws or regulations in your area. The last thing you want is to become attached to your new pet only to find out that you are not allowed to keep him.

Because Green-Cheeked are frequently captive-bred for the pet trade, import and export may not be an issue. Sun Conures, however, are listed as an endangered species and are protected by the Wild Bird Conservation Act of 1992. In order to keep a Sun Conure as a pet, you will need to purchase a bird that can be proven as a captive-bred specimen – you may also need to obtain a captive-bred wildlife permit.

To determine whether you need a permit to purchase and keep a Conure in your area, consult your local council. Keep in mind that if you intend to move from one state to another and plan to take your Conure with you, you might need a permit. All 50 U.S. states require a health certificate issued by a veterinarian for every bird coming into the state.

In many cases, even if a permit is not required to keep a Conure as a pet you may still be required to legally identify the bird. The most common form of identification for live birds is metal leg bands. Leg bands are used to identify individual birds, to connect them to their owners and to prove that the bird was either imported legally or bred domestically. Before you can get a permit (where permits are necessary), you will need to make sure the bird is banded. For specific questions regarding regulations in your area, contact the Fish and Wildlife Service.

b.) Licensing in the U.K.

In the United Kingdom, wild birds are protected under the Wildlife and Countryside Act 1981. This act regulates the capture and killing of wild birds native to the U.K. There are, however, no regulations prohibiting U.K. citizens from keeping non-endangered species of non-native bird such as the Green-Cheeked Conure. You will, however, be required to obtain a permit if you plan to import or export the bird into or out of the U.K.

Before you buy a Conure, however, it would be wise to check with your local council. You may regret it later if you do not check and then find out that there is some sort of regulation in place. If this happens, you may be forced to give up your pet or the government may go so far as to euthanize it.

c.) Licensing Elsewhere

In Australia, there are no regulations regarding the keeping of non-native birds as pets. In fact, there are also 41 species of native bird that can be kept legally without a license. Licensing requirements are very similar in Canada to the U.S. A permit is required to import/export birds to and from the country. Licenses to keep/breed Conures may be necessary depending what region you live in so you will need to contact your local council to make sure.

2.) How Many Should You Buy?

This question is tricky because the answer depends upon the personality of individual birds. In the wild, both Sun Conures and Green-Cheeked Conures live in large flocks of 10 to 30 individuals. This is not practical if you plan to keep Conures as pets, but you may be wondering whether these birds will do better alone or in pairs. Do not assume that keeping two birds together will lessen their need for human affection and interaction – purchasing a second bird is not a short-cut to minimizing the time requirements in caring for a Conure as a pet.

Unfortunately, keeping two Conures together can go horribly wrong if you do not take a few precautions. Many bird owners recommend that if you plan to keep more than one Conure that you give them separate cages but allow them to spend some free time together. This will ensure that the two do not fight with each other in the cage and also increases the chance that they still want to spend time with you. If you do keep more than one Conure, plan to buy two separate cages but keep them within sight of each other and give them some time outside the cage to interact.

3.) Do Conures Make Good Family Pets?

The answer to this question is two-fold – you need to consider whether Conures are good with children and whether or not they can get along with other household pets. While Green-Cheeked Conures are gentler than many other parrots, Sun Conures can still be a little bit nippy. Both species need to be properly socialized if you plan to keep them as a family pet. Regardless, they are likely to bond with one person more than the others and may not seem like much of a "family" pet at times.

Another thing to consider is the fact that Conures require a significant amount of time and attention. This being the case, a Conure may not be the best choice for children. This is not to say that they can't be kept in a home where children are present, but a Conure isn't the ideal pet to give specifically to a child. With proper supervision and preparation, however, mature or older children can certainly be capable of caring for a Conure.

Regarding the issue of keeping Conures with other household pets, the answer to this question is not simple either. Again, it all depends on the temperament and personality of the bird and of the other pet. In most cases, a Conure will not bother a dog or cat but they can produce a lot of noise which may irritate other household pets. You also have to remember that dogs and cats are predatory animals by nature and even if they are gentle around people and other pets, their instincts could kick in and they might chase or even injure the bird. Think carefully before bringing a Conure into a home where other pets are present.

4.) Ease and Cost of Care

Saying that Conures are "difficult" to care for is not exactly accurate. It is more accurate to say that they require a certain degree of care, time and attention in order to thrive. Many people do not realize before buying a bird that they can live to be 20 years or older. If you are not prepared to make this kind of commitment, please do not purchase a Conure as a pet. You also have to realize that Conures can be very social animals and thus require daily human interaction and individual attention from their owners.

In addition to these things, you also need to think about the cost of keeping a Conure as a pet. Before you buy a Conure, think about the cost of the bird itself as well as the price of the proper cage. Once you cover these costs you still have to think about the monthly costs to keep your pet – these costs include food, bedding, chew toys, veterinary care and more. In this section you will learn just what costs you can expect in having a Conure as a pet so you can be fully prepared before you take the leap.

a.) Initial Costs

Some of the initial costs involved in keeping a Conure as a pet include the purchase price of the bird, the cost of the cage

Purchase Price: The purchase price for a Green-Cheeked Conure varies depending where you buy it. If you purchase from a reputable breeder, you should expect to pay between $150 and $500 (£97.50 to £325) for a weaned baby. Sun Conures are a little more expensive, generally costing between $250 and $600 (£162.50 to £390) when purchased from a breeder.

Depending where you live, if you purchase from a pet store you may find the price to be significantly higher. To save on costs, you might want to check out some local parrot rescues in your area. You may be able to adopt an adult or baby Conure for much less than the price of purchasing from a breeder.

Cage Cost: The cost of a cage for Conures depends on the size. These birds are not particularly large, but they do require space in order to thrive. You do not need to purchase a cage large enough to accommodate some of the larger parrot species such as Macaws because you can let your Conure spend some free time outside the cage. In order to get a cage large enough to keep your Conure comfortable, however, you should plan to spend between $150 and $400 (£97.50 to £260).

Chew Toys: Conures, especially Sun Conures, have a tendency to chew on anything they can get. For this reason it is important that you provide them with a collection of chew toys to keep them occupied. These toys are not very expensive but you should plan to have several on hand for when you need them. Costs for a collection of parrot chew toys are generally around $50 (£32.50).

Other Supplies: In addition to the Conure itself, the cage and chew toys you may also want to purchase a few other supplies to have on hand. These supplies may include grooming tools, cleaning supplies and additional cage accessories. The cost for purchasing these items may range from $25 to $100 (£16.25 to £65).

Initial Costs for Conures		
Cost	**Green-Cheeked**	**Sun Conure**
Purchase Price	$150 to $500 (£97.50 to £325)	$250 to $600 (£162.50 to £390)

Cage Cost	$150 and $400 (£97.50 to £260)	$150 and $400 (£97.50 to £260)
Chew Toys	$50 (£32.50)	$50 (£32.50)
Other Supplies	$25 to $100 (£16.25 to £65)	$25 to $100 (£16.25 to £65)
Total	$375 to $1050 (£243.75 to £682.50)	$475 to $1150 (£308.75 to £747.50)

b.) Monthly Costs

After purchasing your Conure, its cage and other initial necessities, you are not off the hook. Every month you will need to budget a certain amount of money for your Conure's food and other needs. Some of the other monthly costs you should plan for include veterinary bills, cage repairs, toy replacements and other unexpected costs.

Cage Lining: For the most part, cage liners will not cost you much per month because you can simply use recycled newspaper. Most newspaper inks are soy-based so they will not harm your Conure. You should be careful when using colored-ink paper, however, because these inks may contain toxins. If your Conure cage has a separate compartment for the cage liner you may not need to worry about this at all.

For the sake of budgeting your costs, plan for a monthly cost of less than $5 (£3.25) for cage lining.

Food: Feeding a Conure is not a terribly significant expense, depending what kind of food you use. A Conure should be offered a varied diet of commercial pellets, seeds, fresh fruits and vegetables. The cost for feeding a Conure is about $25 (£16.25) per month.

Veterinary Costs: Veterinary costs for birds like Conures can be extremely variable. A typical exam may only cost between $50 and $75 (£32.50 to £48.75). If the bird needs tests or medications, however, it can run between $200 and $500 (£130 to £325). It will probably not be necessary to take your Conure to the vet every month, so divide the annual cost of $50 to $500 (£32.50 to £325) by 12 for a monthly budget of about $5 to $42 (£3.25 to £27.30).

Other Costs: Some of the other costs you may need to think about in regard to keeping Conures as pets include repairs to the cage, replacements for food dishes and toys, cleaning supplies and other unexpected costs. Though you may not end up having any of these expenses some months, it is wise to budget about $25 (£16.25) per month for incidentals.

Monthly Costs for Conures		
Cost	Green-Cheeked	Sun Conure
Cage Lining	$5 (£3.25)	$5 (£3.25)
Food	$25 (£16.25)	$25 (£16.25)
Veterinary Costs	$5 to $42 (£3.25 to £27.30)	$5 to $42 (£3.25 to £27.30)
Other Costs	$25 (£16.25)	$25 (£16.25)
Total	$60 to $97 (£39 to £63.05)	$60 to $97 (£39 to £63.05)

5.) Pros and Cons of Conures

Before you buy a Conure, you should take the time to learn the pros and cons of keeping them as pets. All pets have their advantages and disadvantages but if you buy one before you learn the details, you might find yourself ill-prepared and unable to provide your Conure with the care it needs. In this section you will learn the pros and cons of Green-Cheeked Conures and Sun Conures as pets so you can decide whether they are the right choice for you.

Pros of Green-Cheek Conures as Pets:

- Adaptable to a variety of living situations (house, apartment, etc.)
- Big personalities in a small package
- Very affectionate, great family pet
- Quite playful, enjoy playing with toys
- Very intelligent, can be trained simple tricks and limited vocabulary
- Not as loud as other species of parrot
- More interactive and intelligent than many smaller pet bird species

---

Cons of Green-Cheek Conures as Pets:

- May become fearful if not socialized well
- Can be a little nippy, may bite children or inexperienced handlers
- If not properly socialized, may be aggressive or difficult
- Can be noisy as pets (may annoy neighbors)
- May be destructive if left out of the cage unsupervised
- Require significant time and attention (highly social)

Pros of Sun Conures as Pets:

- Very affectionate, often bonds closely with owner
- Big personalities in a small package
- Quite playful, enjoy playing with toys
- Can be taught simple tricks with extensive training
- More interactive than many smaller pet bird species

Cons of Sun Conures as Pets:

- Very loud, not recommended for apartments
- Can be messy, may require extra maintenance
- May become fearful or aggressive if not socialized well

- Can be a little nippy, may bite children or inexperienced handlers
- Can be noisy as pets (may annoy neighbors)
- May be destructive if left out of the cage unsupervised

Chapter Four: Purchasing Conures

If you have made it this far through the book, you have probably decided that a Green-Cheeked or Sun Conure is indeed the right pet for you and your family. Before you rush out to buy one, however, you should take a few things into consideration. Where you buy your bird will have a direct influence on the quality of its breeding and this its overall health. You should take the time to choose a reputable breeder to purchase from and learn to recognize the signs of a healthy Conure so you can be sure the bird you bring home is in ideal condition.

1.) Where to Buy Conures

If, after reading the pros and cons of Conures as pets along with the projected costs of owning them you still feel that these are the right pets for you, you can move on to thinking about where to buy one. There are several options for buying Conures in the U.S. and the U.K. – it is mainly a matter of preference which option you choose. In this section you will learn the benefits of the various options so you can decide which option is best.

a.) Buying in the U.S.

There are three different places you can go to get a Conure in the U.S. – a pet store, a breeder or a bird rescue. All three of these options have their benefits so learn the basics before you buy. A pet store has the advantage of being local and convenient. You cannot, however, be sure about the breeding of the bird so you may end up having to deal with health problems down the line. Many pet stores also mark up the prices of their pets so you could end up spending a significantly larger amount on a pet store Conure than you would purchasing from a breeder.

The main benefit of buying a Conure from a breeder is that you can get the bird while it is still young. Purchasing from a reputable breeder also ensures that the bird was bred well and it may also come with a health guarantee. Keep in mind that not all breeders are experienced in breeding birds – you should take the time to interview breeders before you buy. The price you pay for a Conure from a breeder may vary according to the type of Conure, whether it is a particular color morph, and the age of the bird.

If you like the idea of having a Conure as a pet but do not particularly care to raise one from infancy, adopting from a bird rescue is a good option. Adopting from a bird rescue is also a good option if you cannot commit to the 20- to 30-year lifespan of the average Conure. Unfortunately, many of the Conures that end up in rescues come from owners who did not realize the length of the commitment before they bought their bird. You can not only secure a new pet for yourself in adopting but you can also improve the life of an abandoned bird.

b.) Buying in the U.K.

Your options for buying a Conure in the U.K. are very similar to those in the U.S. Depending where you live, you might be able to find a Conure at your local pet store. If the store does not carry them, you may still be able to get information about breeders in the area. Another way to find local breeders is to check the classifieds in your newspaper or to run an online search.

As is the case in the U.S., adopting a Conure from a bird rescue is another great option. Many Conures available for adoption are already several years old (or older). This means that they are likely already to people, do not need to be hand-fed and may have even been trained to speak or to perform simple tricks. The cost to adopt a Conure is also likely to be much less than the cost of purchasing a baby bird from a breeder.

2.) *How to Select a Healthy Conure*

No matter where you buy your Conure, it is important that you take the time to make sure the bird you bring home is healthy. If you bring home a bird that is not in peak condition, it could cause you a great deal of headache and heartache down the line when you have to put your bird through extensive veterinary care. Buying a healthy Conure starts with picking a reputable breeder. Once you have decided on a breeder you can observe and examine the individual birds to assess their condition.

a.) Things to Look for in a Breeder/Shop

Before purchasing a Conure from anyone, take a few minutes to look around – this applies to both a pet shop and an independent breeder. If the facilities don't look clean or if the animals are obviously not healthy, you don't need to hang around any longer – move on to a place that takes better care of their animals. For more things to look for in a breeder/shop, consult the following list:

- Ask questions to determine how much the breeder knows about the species

- If the breeder or pet shop asks you questions too it is a good sign – it shows that they want their pets to go to the right people

- Take a minute to recognize the difference between normal mess and neglect – birds are messy creatures but there shouldn't be droppings caked on perches or piled on the floor of the cage

- Check to see if clean water and fresh food are available – you should also make sure that the birds are being offered a healthy diet

– The breeder shouldn't be hesitant to give you references

– Ask about a health guarantee – whether you are buying from a breeder or pet store, there should be some sort of health check involved

b.) Picking Out a Healthy Bird

Whether you are buying from a pet store or picking a baby bird out from a breeder, you should take a few minutes to make sure the animal you are bringing home is in optimal condition. Consult the following list for things to check when picking out a bird:

– Make sure the bird is at least 8 to 12 weeks old before buying – a breeder may allow you to visit the babies before they are weaned but don't buy one until it is old enough

– Take a few minutes to assess the personality of the bird – Green-Cheeks in particular are known for being friendly so if the birds are frightened of people they may not be properly socialized

- If the birds are afraid of people or shy away from your touch, it could also be a sign of illness – animals often become defensive when they are sick

- Don't be surprised if the baby birds nibble a bit on your fingers – you should only be worried if they display obvious signs of aggression

- The bird's feathers should be clean and shiny – if the feathers are dull or molting, the bird may not be healthy

- Look for stress bars on the bird's feathers – these bars are black and form during periods of stress (some stress bars are normal but make sure there aren't too many)

- Choose a bird that you connect with – Conures form close bonds with their owners so if you bond with one in particular, stick with it

Chapter Five: Caring for Conures

In order to provide your Conure with the best possible care, it is important that you learn everything you can about them. Conures require a specific habitat in order to thrive and a particular diet to remain healthy. In this chapter you will learn the basics about creating the ideal Conure habitat and diet to keep your bird happy. You will also receive tips for grooming and training your Conure.

1.) *Habitat Requirements*

In the wild, Conures spend their lives in large flocks inhabiting the forested areas of South America. As house pets, however, these birds are typically confined to a cage. In order to make your Conure more comfortable, it is important that you provide him with a cage that gives him room to move around – you should also be sure to incorporate daily time spent outside the cage so he can stretch his wings. In this section you will learn everything there is to know about creating the ideal habitat for your Green-Cheeked or Sun Conure.

a.) Ideal Cage Size

As is true for most pets, when it comes to picking a cage for a Conure the rule to follow is "bigger is better." You must, of course, take into account how much space you have available in your house, but the more room you can give your bird, the better off he will be. The minimum cage dimensions for a Conure are 16x16x18 inches (40.6x40.6x45.7 cm). The less time your Conure spends outside the cage, however, the larger the cage should be. If your bird primarily uses the cage for sleeping, a cage of these dimensions should be fine.

b.) Conure Cage Details

In addition to the size of the cage, you also need to think carefully about the materials from which your cage is built. Though galvanized wire cages are very common for pet birds, they are not ideal – the metal coating on the wire is often zinc which can poison your bird if he chews on it. The ideal cage material is stainless steel because it will hold up under your bird's claws and beak without posing any risk to the bird in terms of toxic coating. Another option is a steel cage coated with powder paint – these cages are less expensive than stainless steel and as long as the paint is non-toxic they are a safe option for Conures.

When choosing your Conure's cage you need to not only think about the dimensions of the cage but also the spacing of the bars. If the spacing is too wide, your Conure could get its head or wing through the bars – if it is too small the bird could get a foot caught in the holes. For Conures, the recommended spacing is about ½ inch (1.25 cm). Most bird cages feature vertical bars rather than mesh-style bars which can easily pose a hazard to birds.

Another detail you need to think about is where you will place your Conure's cage. Because these birds are fairly social by nature, the cage should be kept somewhere they are likely to receive frequent human interaction. The cage should not, however, be in the center of a high-activity zone or your bird may become stressed by the constant noise and activity. Make sure to put the cage in a sunny, draft-free location because birds require a stable temperature in order to thrive – drafts and chills can cause your bird to fall ill.

If you are able to shop around for your Conure's cage, try to find one that has a slide-out tray bottom. You can line the tray with newspaper or some other recycled paper to making cleaning up your bird's droppings easier. These trays are easy to remove and rinse without having to disassemble the entire cage or move your bird to another location. You can also line the tray with a towel if you don't have newspaper because the towel can simply be tossed in the washer to clean it.

c.) Cage Accessories

If you have never owned a pet bird before, you may be tempted to purchase some kind of starter kit that comes with plastic bowls, perches and other accessories. While this may seem like a deal to you, it may not be ideal for your Conure. Keep in mind that birds spend nearly all day everyday on a perch so you should do your best to provide a surface that is comfortable for them! Even though their feet look tough, a Conure's feet are sensitive and they would much rather wrap their toes around a natural tree branch than a piece of plastic.

To save yourself some money, and to make your Conure happy in the process, use branches cut from trees as perches in your bird cage. Make sure to avoid poisonous trees like hemlock but most species including birch, evergreen, alder, maple and willow will do just fine. Only use branches that have not been treated with pesticides – if you aren't sure, bake it in the oven to disinfect it. You can also switch things up by adding a rope perch or cement perch to supplement the wooden perches in your bird's cage.

In addition to perches, you also need to provide your bird with food and water dishes. In most cases, whatever comes with the cage is fine for a little while. Sometimes these dishes are made from cheap plastic that doesn't last long so, if you want something that will hold up over time, go with stainless steel. Another benefit of stainless steel is that it is unbreakable and easy to clean. They may become scratched or dented over time but they still work!

The final accessory your bird cage needs is a collection of toys. Toys do more than just give your bird something to play with – they also help to stimulate the bird mentally and may also help to keep its beak and nails filed down. Rope toys are a good option but you need to keep an eye on them – once they unravel, it is time for a replacement. Avoid toys that have galvanized wire components and don't go for toys that have small holes your bird's beak or toes could get stuck in. Look for toys that are sized appropriately for cockatiels or slightly larger birds and buy a collection so your bird can pick what he likes best.

d.) Sleeping Area for Conures

You may not think about it naturally, but even pet birds like to have some form of shelter in their cage where they can sleep. Something as simple as a cloth tube hung from the ceiling of the cage provides your Conure with a dark area where they can retreat. Young birds are more likely to accept tents or sleeping tubes but it may take some time for older birds to get used to them. Do not be surprised if you find your bird sleeping on the floor of the cage – he will sleep wherever he is most comfortable.

2.) *Feeding Conures*

The key to keeping your Conures healthy is to provide them with a diet that meets all of their nutritional needs. You cannot give a bird a bowl of plain seeds or grain every day and expect it to be healthy – Conures need a varied diet that provides an assortment of vitamins, minerals and other nutrients. In this section, you will learn everything there is to know about your Conure's nutritional needs and how to meet them through a balanced diet of commercial pellets, seeds and other foods.

a.) Nutritional Needs of Conures

Like all animals, Conures require a balance of protein, fat, carbohydrate, vitamins and minerals in order to thrive. If you do not provide your bird with a balanced diet, it could suffer from nutritional deficiencies and may fall ill as a result. The diets of wild and pet birds are divided into categories based on the foods they eat. Conures are considered both granivores (grain- and seed-eating) as well as frugivores (eat fruits and flowers).

A commercial parrot pellet should be the basis of any diet for Conures because it helps to provide rounded nutrition. Conures cannot thrive on a pellet diet alone, however – you will need to offer supplemental foods such as seeds, fruit and some vegetables to keep your bird healthy. Below you will find a breakdown of the nutritional needs for a Green-Cheeked or Sun Conure.

Protein

The specific protein needs of parrots has not been thoroughly researched. It is known, however, that fiber intake is linked to protein needs because with increased fiber in the diet, more protein is lost in the fecal matter. The estimated protein level recommended for adult Conures is between 7 and 12% of the total diet – this number increases for growing hatchlings and egg-laying hens. It is important to make sure that your Conure doesn't get too much protein, however, because this can cause renal problems.

Fat

Dietary fat provides a Conure's body with energy and essential fatty acids which aids in the absorption of certain vitamins and, in hens, contributes to egg yolk formation. The recommendations for fat in a Conure's diet are not specific, but should remain fairly low because too much fat in the diet could lead to obesity or cardiac disease.

Carbohydrate

Carbohydrates are the primary source of energy in a Conure's diet. These nutrients can be found in sugars, starches and cellulose which comes from fats and fibers.

Vitamins

The most important vitamins for a Conure are vitamins A, D, E and K. Vitamin A helps maintain healthy vision, reproduction and growth – it also helps to stimulate the immune system. Vitamin D helps the body to absorb key minerals including calcium and phosphorus. Vitamin E is an antioxidant which helps to improve brain function and works with various minerals in the body. Vitamin K is a water-soluble vitamin which is essential for maintaining healthy blood clotting – unlike other vitamins, it is not stored in the body and must be a regular part of the diet.

Minerals

The most important mineral in a Conure's diet is calcium. Calcium helps to maintain skeletal health and is also necessary for the correct functioning of nerve cells. Fortunately, most Conures are able to get the necessary amount of calcium from a varied diet so they generally do not require supplements. In fact, too much calcium can cause health problems so supplementation is best avoided.

Water

Though water is neither a mineral nor a vitamin, it is still an essential part of your bird's diet. It is important that you provide your Conure with fresh water on a daily basis. Fresh water should be constantly available because it helps to cool and hydrate the body – it is also essential for regulating the elimination of waste and for the digestion and absorption of food.

b.) How Much to Feed

The amount your Conure eats will depend on its age, size and activity level. Generally, it is recommended that you have a bowl of commercial pellets available all the time for your bird. Do not fill the bowl too full, however, because you should keep the pellets in it fresh. You can also mix in a small amount of seeds if the pellet mixture doesn't already contain them. Avoid giving your bird too many sunflower or safflower seeds, however, because these seeds are very high in fat.

As a general rule, your Conure's diet should consist of between 65 and 80% commercial pellets. Fresh vegetables should make up another 15 to 30% of the diet while fruits and seeds fill the remaining portion. Vegetables are an excellent source of vitamins and minerals for birds so you should be sure to offer a variety. Fruits, on the other hand, are high in sugar so they should be offered less frequently. If your bird was raised in a pet store on a seed-based diet, you may need to start him off on a seed-focused diet and slowly work in more pellets.

c.) Types of Food

Aside from their main diet of commercial pellets, Conures enjoy a variety of fruits and vegetables. Consult the following list to determine which fruits and vegetables are safe and recommended for Conures:

Vegetables:

Broccoli	Collard Greens
Beet Greens	Dandelion Greens
Carrots	Endive
Cauliflower	Eggplant
Cooked Red Potato	Green Beans
Cooked Sweet Potato	Kale
Corn	Kohlrabi
Cucumber	Mustard Greens
Parsley	Radishes

Radicchio

Red Beets

Red Pepper

Romaine Lettuce

Sugar Snap Peas

Squash (steamed)

Swiss Chard

Fruits:

Apples

Apricot

Berries

Banana

Cantaloupe

Cherries

Cranberries

Honeydew

Grapefruit

Grapes

Kiwi

Mango

Oranges

Pears

Peaches

Pomegranate

Plums

Papaya

Foods to Avoid:

Avocado

Chocolate

Alcohol

Coffee (caffeinated drinks)

Fruit pits

Table salt

Garlic and onion

Apple seeds

Mushrooms

Junk food

3.) Trimming a Conure's Wings

In most cases, trimming your Conure's wings is less about grooming than it is about safety. Birds that are kept indoors can easily be injured if allowed to exercise their full flying capabilities – in flight, the bird is more likely to run into dangerous objects, to fly through open doors or windows or to escape from the house where it could be injured. Trimming your Conure's feathers won't cause him any pain and it is relatively simple to do.

To start, loosely wrap your bird's head in a towel to keep it from biting you. Even if your Conure is typically gentle it could become frightened, especially if you have never trimmed its wings before. Once the head is secured, carefully cradle the bird in one arm and slightly extend one of the wings. Starting at the outer edge of the wing, count five of the primary feathers and trim them back to a point just under the second layer of feathers on the wings – the second layer of feathers are called the major coverts. By trimming the primary feathers so the ends sit just under the major coverts, it will keep the trimmed edges from irritating your Conure's skin.

Once you have finished trimming the first wing, adjust the bird as necessary to expose the other wing. Trim five of the primary feathers in the same manner. When finished, carefully unwrap the bird's head and allow it to hop down to the ground. If you've trimmed the feathers properly your Conure should be able to control its flight downward but won't be able to achieve enough lift to fly further. If your Conure is able to achieve regular flight, trim another feather or two from each wing.

4.) *Training Conures*

Conures are a type of parrot but they are not able to achieve the same advanced vocabulary that some species can achieve. With extensive training, both Green-Cheeked and Sun Conures can achieve a limited vocabulary and may even be taught to respond to a few simple commands. In most cases, training a Conure is not about teaching tricks – it is about modifying unwanted or inappropriate behaviors such as screaming, biting or other signs of aggression.

a.) Dealing with Problem Behaviors

Before you can learn how to effectively deal with problem behaviors you should familiarize yourself with some of the methods that *don't* work. Inexperienced parrot owners often make the mistake of yelling at their parrots in an effort to correct their behavior – not only is this ineffective but it could also damage your relationship with your parrot, causing him to develop more behavioral problems. Squirting the bird with water, banging on the cage and hitting the bird are other methods that do not work.

In order to fix problem behaviors you need to understand them. In many cases, problem behaviors are completely natural or instinctual behaviors on the parrot's part – they are only a problem because they interfere with your life or in your interaction with the parrot. Vocalization is a natural parrot behavior and your parrot is likely to become more vocal if he doesn't receive adequate attention or care. You may also unwittingly reinforce problem behaviors by giving your parrot a treat to make him be quiet – this only serves to teach the parrot that he will be fed if he makes noise.

To change your Conure's behavior, you need to take a minute to realize why he is doing it. If your parrot isn't used to being handled, he may bite you – if you immediately put him back in the cage, you are doing exactly what he wants. Learn to identify your parrot's goal in certain behaviors and make a conscious effort not to reinforce problem behaviors. Over time, your parrot will display the problem behaviors less frequently if he stops being rewarded for them.

b.) Teaching Conures to Talk

Training a Conure to speak is not something you can do overnight but, with consistent effort, it can be achieved. You must first realize that it is impractical to expect your Conure to be able to repeat complex sentences – even if you can get your Conure to repeat words, his voice may be difficult to understand. Below you will find several techniques to use in teaching your Conure to speak:

- Repeat a single word or phrase several times throughout every interaction you have with the bird

- If your bird doesn't pick up on the word or phrase, try another one

- Keep your tone upbeat and energetic when training your Conure to speak – that way he is more likely to stay engaged

- Give your Conure rewards when he begins to speak to teach him to repeat the behavior

- Use your training to keep your Conure from screaming – if you reward the bird for talking rather than screaming, he will eventually learn

Chapter Six: Breeding Conures

The breeding process for Sun Conures and Green-Cheeked Conures is fairly similar. There are, however, a few key differences. In this chapter you will learn the basics of breeding Conures and raising the chicks. When applicable, you will find differences between the two species noted. After reading this chapter you should have enough knowledge to begin breeding Conures on your own.

1.) Basic Breeding Info

Most Conure breeders recommend that you do not begin
breeding the birds until they are at least one year old. For
Green-Cheeked Conures, this coincides with the average
age of sexual maturity. Sun Conures, however, may take a
little longer – the typical age of sexual maturity for this
species is around 2 years.

It is true of both species that the sex of the bird cannot be
determined by appearance alone. Thus, if you plan to breed
Conures, you will need to take the bird in for DNA sexing.
There may be subtle differences in appearance between the
sexes in regard to head shape, feet color or vent size – these
methods aren't as reliable as DNA sexing, however.

The incubation periods and clutch sizes for these two
species of Conure vary slightly. In Green-Cheeked Conures,
the average clutch size is 4 to 6 while, in Sun Conures, it is 3
to 5. Most Conures are capable of producing two clutches
per year, especially once they have been bred a few times.
In Sun Conures, the incubation period for eggs is generally
around 23 days while Green-Cheeked Conures may take a
day or two longer.

2.) *The Breeding Process*

Breeding Conures is not especially difficult to achieve – you simply have to find a compatible pair. If you know for sure that you plan to breed your Conures, your best bet is to purchase a breeding pair from a breeder. This ensures that the birds have already been DNA sexed and that they get along. Though Conures are not as picky as some parrots in regard to their mates, you will have much greater success in breeding if the two birds are compatible.

If you have not purchased a breeding pair from a breeder, it may simply be a matter of trial and error. If the pair bonds well, they may begin to perch very close to each other and might feed each other as well. One or both of the birds may begin to display sexual interest in the other and they may begin building a nest. At this point, you will need to provide your Conures with an adequate nest box in which they can lay and incubate their eggs.

Conures that are preparing for breeding need to be separated from other birds. If you have several Conures in a large aviary, you will need to move the breeding pair to a separate breeding cage. In the cage you will need to provide a nest box where the female can lay and tend to the eggs. The minimum dimensions for this nest box are 12x12x12 inches (30.5x30.5x30.5 cm) and the box should be made of sturdy plywood.

Once you have built the next box you will need to line it with about two inches of nesting material on the bottom. The ideal nesting materials to use are shredded newspaper, untreated sawdust or clean straw. In some cases, the female Conure will move the nesting material aside and lay her eggs directly on the floor of the box. As long as the female continues to care for the eggs, this should not be a problem.

In fact, your Conures are unlikely to let you anywhere near the eggs during the incubation period.

While your female Conure is incubating the eggs, the male will typically feed her. This is why it is especially important that the pair be bonded before mating. Prior to breeding it is important to feed the female Conure a diet high in calcium, protein and vitamins. This will ensure that the shells of the eggs are thick enough to protect the babies before they hatch and that the adult birds stay strong to care for the hatchlings. After the eggs hatch, you can supplement the adults' diet with soft foods like apples and sprouted seeds which will be easy for them to regurgitate to feed their young.

3.) Raising the Babies

When the female Conure is almost ready to lay her eggs, she will begin losing feathers on her chest. This bald patch is referred to as a "brood patch" and it allows the female to more efficiently transfer her body heat to the eggs to keep them warm. It may take several days for the female to lay her eggs and it will be another 22 to 25 days until they hatch. Once the babies hatch you will need to decide whether to raise them by hand or to let the parents care for the chicks. Many breeders opt for a combination of the two – feeding the chicks by hand but leaving them with their parents for the rest of the time.

Conure hatchlings are very small when they first emerge from the egg. Green-Cheeked Conures weigh an average of 0.1 oz. (5g) while Sun Conures weigh around 0.2 oz. (6g) at birth. Once they hatch, the chicks should grow fairly quickly and they will develop their first pin feathers by 4 weeks of age. If you plan to let the parents raise the chicks, they will continue to feed them until they are about 6 to 8 weeks old.

It is important to realize that the rearing method you choose for your baby Conures may affect their temperament. If you choose to let the adults raise the chicks, the chicks are likely to become imprinted to the parents and may not be as tame as a result. Parent-raised chicks tend to be better for breeding stock than for pets. Hand-raised chicks, on the other hand, require more time and effort to raise. On the upside, they are more likely to imprint on their human caretakers and will be tamer.

If you plan to hand-raise your chicks, you can remove them from the nest any time after hatching. It is recommended, however, that you wait to do so until they are 3 or 4 weeks old. Hand-raised chicks learn to become very comfortable with people and are often very affectionate and playful with their human companions. You must realize, however, that hand-raising Conure chicks is very time-consuming and you must be ready to dedicate a great deal of effort to the task in order to do it well.

Hand-raised chicks must be fed a special formula by syringe every few hours around the clock. Without the parents present to keep the chicks warm, you will need to keep them in a brooder. Hand-raising can take its toll on the chicks so the longer you wait to remove them from the nest, the stronger and more likely to survive they will be. Older chicks will also require less feeding than new hatchlings.

Once the chicks reach 4 weeks of age they should have developed most of their first pin feathers. By 6 to 8 weeks of age, they should be fully weaned. Sometime during that period, around 7 weeks of age, the hatchlings should become fledglings. This simply means that the birds have begun to acquire the feathers they need to maintain flight. At this point the birds will start to stray further from the nest to test their wings. Before you know it, they will have developed their adult feathers and will have become beautiful adult Conures like their parents.

Chapter Seven: Keeping Conures Healthy

Generally, Conures are hardy and healthy birds. Like all pets, however, they are prone to illness from time to time. In this chapter you will learn about the health conditions common in Conures as well as the recommended treatments. You will also receive valuable tips about preventing illness in your Conures. Some of the common health problems covered in this book include:

- Aspergillosis

- Psittacine Beak and Feather Syndrome (PBFD)

- Chlaymydiosis

- Conure Bleeding Syndrome

- Giardia

- Papillomatosis

- Polyoma

- Proventricular Dilation Disease (PDD)

- Psittacine Poxvirus

- Pacheco's Disease

You will learn more about these diseases in detail in the next section. Keep in mind that many of these diseases can be very serious – it is recommended that you seek veterinary care for treatment.

1.) *Common Health Problems*

Though Conures are typically healthy and hardy birds, like any other animal they are prone to falling ill at some point. In this section you will learn about the causes, symptoms and treatments of the ten most common illnesses affecting Conures. The more you know about these diseases, the more quickly you will be able to identify them and the sooner you will be able to get the treatment your bird needs in order to recover.

Aspergillosis

Known as one of the most common causes of respiratory distress in birds, aspergillosis is caused by a fungal infection of the genus *Aspergillus*. This fungus can be found naturally in the environment and may already be present in the respiratory tract of healthy birds. When the bird's immune system is suppressed by stress, malnutrition of concurrent disease, the spores may spread and cause respiratory distress.

Some of the symptoms of aspergillosis include reduced energy levels, weight loss, exercise intolerance and decreased appetite. These subtle symptoms can go on for months at a time, slowly progressing to labored breathing, respiratory noises or open-mouthed breathing. These signs indicate severe respiratory stress and should be treated by a veterinarian immediately.

Though diagnosis of the disease can be tricky, aspergillosis is treatable. Anti-fungal medications are typically administered and continues for at least 6 weeks. In extreme cases, surgical intervention may be needed to remove granulomas which may be blocking the airway. The prognosis for birds infected with this disease varies depending on the severity – if it is diagnosed early and treated promptly, however, the prognosis is generally good.

Cause: fungal infection of the genus *Aspergillus*
Symptoms: reduced energy levels, weight loss, exercise intolerance and decreased appetite; labored breathing, respiratory noises or open-mouthed breathing in severe cases
Treatment: anti-fungal medications

Psittacine Beak and Feather Syndrome (PBFD)

Thought to be specific to psittacine species of bird, PBFD is caused by a virus belonging to the *Circoviridae* family. This disease is often fatal in young birds and older birds that survive the disease are often thought to be carriers. Transmission of the disease occurs through direct contact with infected birds or through contact with contaminated feces or feather dander. PBFD can also be transmitted through contact with contaminated surfaces.

Some of the symptoms of this deadly disease include loss of feathers, shedding of developing feathers in young birds, loss of powder down, overgrown beak and symmetrical lesions on the beak. In the later stages of the disease, weight loss and depression may also occur. Unfortunately, there is no known treatment for this disease. Spread of the disease can be prevented by isolating infected birds and testing equipment for contamination.

Cause: virus belonging to the *Circoviridae* family
Symptoms: loss of feathers, shedding of developing feathers in young birds, loss of powder down, overgrown beak and symmetrical lesions on the beak
Treatment: no known treatment for this disease; spread of the disease can be prevented by isolating infected birds

Chlaymydiosis

Also known as psittacosis, chlaymydiosis is an infectious disease caused by an atypical bacterium called *Chlamydophila psittaci*. This disease has been known to cause a wide variety of symptoms including discharge from the nose and eyes, sneezing or coughing, weight loss, loss of appetite, discolored droppings and diarrhea. What makes this disease difficult to diagnose is its waxing and waning nature – birds may go through periods of deteriorating condition alternating with normal periods.

Unfortunately, this disease can be transferred to humans. Generally, this disease causes flu-like symptoms in people and it can progress to pneumonia which may become very severe and life-threatening. The good news is that chlaymydiosis is treatable in birds. Once a diagnosis has been made, antibiotics are usually administered by injection once a week for 4 weeks. There is no vaccine to protect your bird against the disease but you can prevent it by quarantining new birds and having them tested by a veterinarian.

Cause: atypical bacterium called *Chlamydophila psittaci*

Symptoms: discharge from the nose and eyes, sneezing or coughing, weight loss, loss of appetite, discolored droppings and diarrhea

Treatment: antibiotics are usually administered by injection once a week for 4 weeks

Conure Bleeding Syndrome

Often shortened to CBS, conure bleeding syndrome is most common in baby Conures, particularly Sun Conures, Nandays and Blue-Crowned Conures. This disease manifests in the form of symptoms similar to those of toxicosis – these symptoms may include recurrent bleeding episodes, weakness or drowsiness, external or internal bleeding and eventual death.

The causes of this condition are not definitive but some potential causes include retrovirus, dietary insufficiency or abnormal clotting mechanisms. Treatment for this disease can be prescribed by a vet and typically takes the form of vitamin K or vitamin D3 injections – calcium supplements and antibiotics may also be recommended. This disease can often be prevented by providing a balanced diet that includes calcium- and vitamin K-rich foods.

Cause: retrovirus, dietary insufficiency or abnormal clotting mechanisms

Symptoms: recurrent bleeding episodes, weakness or drowsiness, external or internal bleeding and eventual death

Treatment: vitamin K or vitamin D3 injections – calcium supplements and antibiotics may also be recommended

Giardia

Giardia is a parasite that can be found in water – once ingested it tends to inhabit the intestinal tract of birds and other animals. Once the bird has been infected, it can pass the disease along through its stool. What makes this parasite so dangerous is that it is protected by an outer shell which enables it to survive for long periods of time outside the body of its host.

Unfortunately, cases of giardia are often asymptomatic – in those cases in which symptoms occur, they may be so mild that they go unnoticed. Some symptoms of this disease include intense itching, licking non-food items, chronic diarrhea, lethargy and weight loss. If not properly treated, giardia can eventually lead to death.

The bad news is that giardia can be difficult to diagnose. Examination of fecal smears is required to make a diagnosis but the parasites are passed intermittently, so they may not appear in every sample. The good news is that giardia is a treatable condition. In most cases, antiprotozoal medications are prescribed and administered through hand-feeding and crop needle for about 5 days. To prevent re-infection, the bird should be switched to a water bottle rather than a water bowl to avoid contamination from droppings.

Cause: a parasite that can be found in water
Symptoms: intense itching, licking non-food items, chronic diarrhea, lethargy and weight loss
Treatment: antiprotozoal medications

Papillomatosis

This disease can be very scary for parrot owners because it causes the formation of wart-like tumors. Luckily, these tumors are benign (non-cancerous) but they can give you quite a scare. Papillomatotis is caused by a virus belonging to the family papovavirus, the same family to which the polyoma virus belongs.

In most cases, these warts develop on the non-feathered skin of the parrot, commonly on the feet, legs, jaw, beak, neck and eyelids. It is possible for these warts to form in the gastrointestinal tract as well – these formations are much harder to diagnose and treat. The most common treatment for this condition is removal of the warts through cautery. In some cases, multiple treatments may be needed and the warts may recur because they are caused by a virus.

Cause: virus belonging to the family papovavirus
Symptoms: formation of wart-like tumorson the non-feathered skin of the parrot
Treatment: removal of the warts through cautery

Polyoma

Also called avian polyomavirus, this disease is one of the most feared viral infections seen in pet birds. Unfortunately, this virus is also frequently misunderstood because birds can easily be infected then become carriers, passing the virus on to other birds without showing any symptoms themselves. Polyomavirus typically infects young birds, but it can affect older birds as well. Transmission is thought to occur through contact with contaminated feces and feather dander from infected birds.

The common signs of this disease vary depending on the age of the infected bird. Young birds typically exhibit signs of depression, regurgitation, diarrhea, loss of appetite and dehydration. In many cases, young birds affected by the virus die within 12 to 48 hours of developing symptoms. Another form of the disease has been known to cause weight loss, recurrent infections and poor feather condition.

Polyomavirus can be difficult to treat because infected birds often do not exhibit symptoms until it is too late. The disease can only be confirmed by blood test or, post-mortem, by tissue examination. Though there are ways to identify disease there are currently no treatments against it. Luckily, a vaccine for avian polyomavirus is available – it is best administered while the bird is young then a booster should be given 2 to 3 weeks later. In some cases, birds exhibit yellowing or discoloration at the site of the vaccine administration but these side effects usually go away within 3 to 6 weeks.

Cause: contact with contaminated feces and feather dander from infected birds
Symptoms: depression, regurgitation, diarrhea, loss of appetite and dehydration

Treatment: no treatment available; vaccine is available and should be administered while bird is young

Proventricular Dilation Disease (PDD)

Proventricular dilation disease, or PDD, most often affects macaws which is why it is also referred to as macaw wasting disease. Despite being more common in macaws, this disease has been known to affect many species of parrot and it can be extremely devastating, even fatal, in a short period of time. Unfortunately, the symptoms of PDD are not unique to the disease – they can easily be confused for other conditions including lead poisoning, fungal infections or bacterial infections. Some of the symptoms of PDD include regurgitation, weight loss, loss of coordination, depression, pendulous crops and sudden death.

It can be very difficult to diagnose this disease in parrots that are still living. Diagnosis can be confirmed through blood tests and bacterial/fungal cultures but the results may not be entirely conclusive. The cause of the disease was debated for a number of years but has finally been identified as a virus called avian bornavirus. Though the cause of the disease is now known, treatment still has varying rates of success. The disease can be managed through feeding easily digestible food and, on some cases, by administering anti-inflammatory drugs.

Cause: avian bornavirus

Symptoms: regurgitation, weight loss, loss of coordination, depression, pendulous crops and sudden death

Treatment: disease can be managed through feeding easily digestible food and, on some cases, by administering anti-inflammatory drugs

Psittacine Poxvirus

Also simply referred to as poxvirus, this disease is particularly common in birds housed outdoors and young parrots. Poxvirus is transmitted through ingestion or inhalation of the virus – it can also enter the body through an open wound or sore. Once the disease has been contracted, it typically goes through an incubation period of 5 to 10 days before symptoms manifest.

There are several different forms of the disease but the type known to commonly affect parrots is referred to as "wet pox". The first symptom of this disease in parrots is often conjunctivitis, or itching, inflammation or discharge of the eyes. This may be followed by the formation of lesions on the mouth and tongue – these lesions may even extend down into the esophagus. This disease can't be treated medically, but supportive care may improve the bird's chances of recovery. Vitamin A injections may help to provide relief for symptoms affecting the skin and mouth while antibiotics or antifungal medications may be used to treat secondary infections.

Cause: through ingestion or inhalation of the virus – it can also enter the body through an open wound or sore
Symptoms: conjunctivitis followed by the formation of lesions on the mouth and tongue
Treatment: no medical treatment available; Vitamin A injections may help to provide relief and antibiotics or antifungal medications may be used to treat secondary infections

Pacheco's Disease

Also known as Pacheco's herpes virus, this disease is highly contagious and can be fatal. This disease is caused by viruses of the herpes viridae family which are primarily known to infect the lymphatic tissue, skin cells and nerve cells. What makes this disease so contagious is the fact that the virus can start shedding in the feces of infected birds in as few as 3 days. The virus is not known to affect birds of a certain age more than any other and it can quickly work its way through an aviary.

Pacheco's disease is typically transmitted through contaminated discharge and feces. In some cases, a parrot may be a carrier of the disease without showing any symptoms. When symptoms do manifest, it is typically in the form of lethargy, diarrhea, anorexia, conjunctivitis and tremors. Unfortunately, the most commonly used treatment for this disease, Acyclovir, can also cause kidney damage in birds. Your best bet is to prevent the spread of the disease by isolating new birds and disinfecting all contaminated surfaces.

Cause: viruses of the herpesviridae family; transmitted through contaminated discharge and feces

Symptoms: lethargy, diarrhea, anorexia, conjunctivitis and tremors

Treatment: Acyclovir - may cause kidney damage; prevention through isolation and sanitation is recommended

2.) *Preventing Illness*

Dealing with illness in your Conure can be heartbreaking, especially if the disease turns fatal. Though you can't prevent your parrot from ever coming into contact with disease, there are things you can do to lessen the chances. In this section you will learn to identify some of the most common signs of illness in parrots and will also receive advice regarding parrot vaccinations.

a.) Signs of Illness in Parrots

In order to have the best chance of treating your parrot's illness in a timely manner you should learn to identify the signs of illness. The sooner you realize that your bird is sick, the sooner you can make a diagnosis and start proper treatment. The following list includes some of the common signs of illness in parrots:

- Change in color or consistency of droppings
- Abnormal breathing or sleep patterns
- Change in behavior, sudden or severe
- Lessening of normal activity (talking, preening, play)
- Reduced energy levels

- Discharge from eyes or beak

- Drinking more water than usual

- Palpable lumps or swelling in the body

- Dull feathers, unclean appearance

- Vomiting or weight loss

- Hunched over or fluffed-up posture

- Drooping tail, head or wings

- Excessive plucking or picking of feathers

Keep in mind that your parrot may not necessarily show any visible signs of illness. Your best bet may be to look for changes in behavior, posture, eating habits or activity level. If you notice any significant changes, consult your veterinarian as soon as possible.

b.) Vaccines for Parrots

If you have ever owned a cat or dog, you may be tempted to think that birds also require regular vaccinations. The reality is that there are very few vaccinations available for pet birds and even those that are may not be recommended for use. The only vaccine that is used with any regularity for parrots like Conures is the polyoma virus vaccine.

The polyoma virus can quickly become fatal without ever showing symptoms which is why vaccination against it is tempting. Unfortunately, the efficacy of the vaccine is controversial so not all veterinarians are willing to administer it. There are cases, however, in which the vaccine has proven effective, particularly in very young birds. After first receiving the vaccination, the bird will need a booster after 2 to 3 weeks.

Chapter Eight: Conure Care Sheet

After reading this book you should have answers to nearly all of your questions regarding Conures as pets. If you have a quick question, however, you may not want to skim through the bulk of the content to find the answer. For your convenience, included in this chapter is a summary of the most important facts regarding the care, keeping and breeding of Conures. You will also find information about bird-proofing your home to prevent damage.

1.) Basic Information

Classification: subfamily Arinae, tribe Arini

Species Name: *Pyrrhura molinae* (Green-Cheeked Conure); *Aratinga solstitialis* (Sun Conure)

Distribution: South America

Habitat (Green-Cheeked Conure): primarily forest and woodland; typically found at treetop level

Habitat (Sun Conure): savanna, coastal forests, foothills

Social Groups: typically flocks of 10 to 20, up to 30

Size: 10 inches (26 cm) Green-Cheeked Conure; 12 inches (30 cm) Sun Conure

Weight: 2.0 to 2.8 oz. (60 to 80 g) Green-Cheeked Conure; 4 oz. (110 g) Sun Conure

Primary Coloration: green body, blue wings, maroon tail (Green-Cheeked Conure); yellow body, orange chest and head, green tail and wing tips (Sun Conure)

Noise Level: moderate (Green-Cheeked Conure); very loud (Sun Conure)

Training: can be taught limited vocabulary, can imitate humans to some degree, may be taught simple tricks

Temperament (Green-Cheeked Conure): playful and affectionate, enjoys being held

Temperament (Sun Conure): can be inquisitive, demands a great deal of attention

Lifespan: 15 to 30 years

2.) Cage Set-up Guide

Minimum Size: 16x16x18 inches (40.6x40.6x45.7 cm)
Cage Materials: stainless steel or powder-coated steel
Cage Location: sunny, draft-free area; place where frequent human interaction is likely
Cage Properties: vertical bars, spacing about ½ inch (1.25 cm), sliding tray bottom
Accessories: wooden, rope or cement perch; stainless steel food and water dish
Toys: toys sized for cockatiels or slightly larger birds; avoid small holes and galvanized wire elements
Sleeping Area: cloth tube or tent hung from cage ceiling

3.) Feeding Guide

Diet Type: granivore, frugivore
Nutritional Needs: protein, fat, carbohydrate, vitamins, minerals and water
Water Needs: fresh water available at all times; refresh daily
Commercial Pellets: small amount available at all times; refresh daily
Dietary Breakdown: 65 to 80% pellets; 15 to 30% vegetables, remaining fruits and seeds
Foods to Avoid: chocolate, onions/garlic, caffeine, table salt, junk food, avocado, alcohol, fruit pits, mushrooms

4.) Breeding Facts Summary

Sexual Maturity (Green-Cheeked): about 1 year

Sexual Maturity (Sun Conures): around 2 years

Incubation Period: 22 to 25 days

Average Clutch: 4 to 6 eggs(Green-Cheeked), 3 to 5 eggs (Sun Conure)

Clutches Per Year: usually 2

Nest Box Material: strong plywood

Minimum Dimensions: 12x12x12 inches (30.5x30.5x30.5cm)

Entrance Hole: 3-inch (7.6 cm) diameter

Nesting Material: shredded newspaper, clean straw, untreated saw dust

Hatchling Weight: 0.1 oz. (5g) Green-Cheeked; 0.2 oz. (6g) Sun Conure

Develop Feathers: about 4 weeks

Weaning Age: 6 to 8 weeks

Fledgling Age: 7 to 8 weeks

5.) Bird-Proofing Tips

Bird-proofing your home is as much about protecting your home from your bird as it is about protecting your bird from the potential dangers present in your home. When bird-proofing your home, be sure to take the following tips into account:

- Cover outlets with plastic covers to prevent electrocution

- Keep all doors and windows securely closed and cover them with drapes or blinds while your Conure is out of the cage

- Clip your bird's wings to keep him from flying too far or too quickly

- Keep your Conure's cage in a warm area away from drafts as well as fans and heaters

- Make sure to keep electrical cords out of your bird's reach – do not leave him alone in a room with electrical appliances

- Cover all ducts and air vents to prevent your bird from getting into them

- Always supervise time your bird spends with children or other pets to prevent injury

- Keep all household chemicals including cleaning products secured in cabinets your bird can't get into

- Clean up all spills and uneaten food to keep your bird from getting into it

- Keep foods that are toxic to birds out of reach – this includes chocolate, avocado, garlic, onions and coffee

- Smoke can be extremely dangerous for birds so avoid smoking in the house

- Make sure any items your bird comes into contact with (especially those he may chew on) are not made from dangerous heavy metals like zinc or lead

- Avoid using scented candles, potpourri and perfumes around your bird

- Be aware that certain light bulbs can become very hot – keep lamps covered with shades

- Make sure to keep your bird away from the food and cages of other pets

- Turn off all ceiling fans and table fans when your bird is out of the cage

- Always check when you close the door to a room or cabinet to make sure your bird doesn't become trapped inside

Chapter Nine: Common Mistakes New Owners Make

If you have never owned a Conure before, or even a pet bird at all, you may be prone to making a few mistakes at first. All new bird owners are subject to a bit of a learning curve but if you do not learn quickly, your Conure could suffer the consequences. In this chapter, you will learn about some of the most common mistakes made by inexperienced Conure owners so you can avoid making them yourself.

Two Birds in the Same Cage

When it comes to pets, the rule is often "two is better than one." In reality, this motto doesn't always play out for the better. Depending on the personalities of your Conures, two birds may not get along if you keep them in the same cage. Of course, it is possible that your birds will get along just great and enjoy spending time together. The opposite is also possible, however – they may not get along at all and you may find yourself needing to separate them later.

If you plan to keep two Conures in the same home, you would be wise to buy them separate cages. Though Conures are social birds in the wild, they do like to have their own space. By keeping your Conures in separate cages, you can also ensure that they will be more likely to bond with you, their human companion. You can certainly allow your Conures to spend time together outside the cage – in fact, it is recommended that you do so. For your own sake – and for your neighbors' – it is best to keep the birds in their own cages during down time to prevent noisy disagreements.

Keeping Sun Conures in an Apartment

Green-Cheeked Conures are known for their playful
personalities – they are also known for being slightly better
behaved and less noisy than other parrot breeds. This is not
the case for Sun Conures, however – they can be very loud
birds, especially if they do not get the attention they crave.
For this reason, it is not a good idea to keep a Sun Conure in
an apartment or condo building. You may not mind the
occasional noise your bird makes, but your neighbors
might. If your building has a no-pet clause, you would be
foolish to think you could get away with keeping a Sun
Conure without anyone noticing.

Improper Diet – Too Many Seeds

Seeds are an important part of a Conure's diet – for many birds, it is the best part! You can, however, give your Conure too many seeds. It is important to realize that some seeds have a fairly high oil content. This means that their fat content is also fairly high. If you feed your Conure too many seeds, he could end up gaining an unhealthy amount of weight. It is better to use seeds as an occasional treat than as a staple of your bird's diet.

Not Purchasing From a Reputable Source

When it comes to buying a Conure for a pet, you should never let price dictate your decision regarding where to buy. You may be able to find a bird for $100 or less but you can't be sure that the breeder is knowledgeable or that the bird itself is in good condition. The only exception to this rule is in the case of adopting from a bird rescue. When adopting from a rescue you can expect the price of the bird to be lower but you do have to keep in mind that the bird may have come from a less-than-ideal situation and could suffer from emotional or behavioral problems.

Keeping a Conure as a pet is not inexpensive and the costs definitely start to pile up when you have to take your bird to the vet. Reputable breeders select their breeding stock very carefully from the healthiest birds available – this ensures that the babies stand the best chance of being healthy when you take them home. If you cut corners and purchase from a questionable source just to save some cash, you may end up spending more money in the long run on costly vet bills.

Not Having a Vet Picked Out

Even if your Conure seems to be in ideal condition when you bring it home, that doesn't guarantee he will stay that way. Before your bird even needs a vet it would be wise for you to pick one out. Not all veterinarians are trained or experienced in caring for birds so you might have to do a little looking around. In the event that something happens and you need to get care for your Conure quickly, if you don't have a vet already chosen you may end up taking him to a veterinary hospital where you may be charged twice the amount (or more) that a regular vet would charge.

Mistaking Eaten Seeds for Uneaten Seeds

While seeds should not be the staple of your bird's diet, they do play an important role in his nutrition. If you have never had a bird before, you may not realize that they do not simply eat the seed whole – they use their beaks to crack open the shell and eat the tender meat inside. If you peek into your parrot's cage and see that his bowl is still full of seeds, take a second look – they may just be the empty shells leftover from eaten seeds.

Chapter Ten: Relevant Websites

In this chapter you will find a variety of resources to help answer questions about Conures that you may still have after reading this book. Here you will find resources for both the U.S. and U.K. regarding the following subjects:

Food for Conures

Care for Conures

Health Info for Conures

General Info about Conures

Training Conures

1.) Food Resources for Conures

In this section you will find a variety of resources to help answer your questions about feeding Conures. Here you will find websites regarding the proper diet, feeding amount and types of treats for Conures.

United States Websites:

"Diet." SunConure.com. <http://sunconure.com/diet>

"What Do Green-Cheeked Conures Eat?" The Majestic Parrot. <http://www.themajesticparrot.com/green-cheeked-conures.html>

"FAQ: Feeding Green Cheeks." The Green Cheek Conure Home Page. <http://gcch.tripod.com/faq/faq6.html>

"Green Cheek Conure Diet." PawNation. <http://animals.pawnation.com/green-cheek-conure-diet>

United Kingdom Websites:

"How to Convert Your Parrot to a Pellet Diet." BirdTrader.co.uk. <http://www.birdtrader.co.uk/bird_advice/how-to-convert-your-parrot-to-a-pellet-diet>

"Breeds and their Needs – Conures." Lakeland Bird Keepers.
<http://www.lakelandbirdkeepers.co.uk/photogallery/breeds_their_needs_Conures.htm>

"Conures." Conure.co.uk.
<http://www.conure.co.uk/Conuresx.html>

2.) Care Resources for Conures

In this section you will find a variety of resources to help answer your questions about caring for Conures. Here you will find websites regarding general Conure care as well as information about cages, perches and more.

United States Websites:

"Sun Conure." World Parrot Trust. <http://www.parrots.org/index.php/encyclopedia/captivest atus/sun_conure/>

"Green-Cheeked Conure Care." The Majestic Parrot. <http://www.themajesticparrot.com/green-cheeked-conures.html>

"Green-Cheeked Conure." World Parrot Trust. <http://www.parrots.org/index.php/encyclopedia/captivest atus/green_cheeked_conure/>

United Kingdom Websites:

"How to Build a Homemade Bird Perch." BirdTrader.co.uk. <http://www.birdtrader.co.uk/bird_advice/how-to-build-a-homemade-bird-perch/435>

"The Best Cage for Your Bird." ProblemParrots.co.uk.
<http://www.problemparrots.co.uk/cages.php>

"How to Trim a Conure's Feathers." BirdTrader.co.uk.
<http://www.birdtrader.co.uk/bird_advice/how-to-trim-a-conure-s-feathers/395>

"Pet Parrot Care Tips." BirdTrader.co.uk.
<http://www.birdtrader.co.uk/bird_advice/pet-parrot-care>

3.) *Health Info Resources for Conures*

In this section you will find a variety of resources to help answer your questions about health information for Conures. Here you will find websites regarding common illnesses, treatment and veterinary care advice for Conures.

United States Websites:

"Bird Medical Conditions." BirdChannel.com.
<http://www.birdchannel.com/diagnostics/default.aspx>

"The Conure." The Caged Bird Courier.
<http://www.yourparrotcage.com/parrot_newsletter/Febuary2011.html>

"Sun Conure Birds." BirdChannel.com.
<http://www.birdchannel.com/bird-species>

United Kingdom Websites:

"Proventricular Dilation Disease (PDD) or Macaw Wasting Disease." BirdTrader.co.uk.
<http://www.birdtrader.co.uk/bird_advice/proventricular-dilatation-disease-pdd-or-macaw-was/515>

"Illnesses and Vets List." ProblemParrot.co.uk.
<http://www.problemparrots.co.uk/illnesses.php>

"How to Treat and Prevent Conure Bleeding Syndrome."
BirdTrader.co.uk.
<http://www.birdtrader.co.uk/bird_advice/how-to-treat-and-prevent-the-conure-bleeding-syndr/490>

4.) *General Info Resources for Conures*

In this section you will find a variety of resources to help answer your general questions about Conures. Here you will find websites regarding the native habitat of Conures, their personalities and different species.

United States Websites:

"Sun Conure." CentralPets.com.
<http://www.centralpets.com/animals/birds/parrots/prt1298.html>

"Green-Cheeked Conure Birds." BirdChannel.com.
<http://www.birdchannel.com/bird-species>

"General Information." SunConure.com.
<http://sunconure.com/general.html>

"Green-Cheeked Conure." Dallas Zoo.
<http://www.dallaszoo.com/animals-birds/green-cheeked-conure/>

"All About Conures." Nikki Moustaki.
<http://betterwords.typepad.com/birdvice/2009/01/conures-all-about-conures.html>

United Kingdom Websites:

"Conures: Green Cheek Conure." BirdTrader.co.uk.
<http://www.birdtrader.co.uk/breed/conures-green-cheek-conure-/32>

"All About Conures." ProblemParrots.co.uk.
<http://www.problemparrots.co.uk/conures.php>

"Conures: Sun Conure." BirdTrader.co.uk.
<http://www.birdtrader.co.uk/breed/conures-sun-conure/59>

5.) *Training Resources for Conures*

In this section you will find a variety of resources to help answer your questions about training Conures. Here you will find websites regarding how to deal with noise, how to train your Conure to speak and tips for dealing with problem behaviors in Conures.

United States Websites:

"Conures." GoodBirdInc.com. <http://www.goodbirdinc.com/parrot-profiles-conures.html>

"Behavior and Training." Conure Community. <http://conurecommunity.com/behavior>

Wilson, Liz. "Managing Parrot Behavior." Canadian Parrot Symposium. <http://www.silvio-co.com/cps/articles/1999/1999lwilson1.htm>

"Training Your Conure Parrot to Obey You." BirdTricks.com. <http://www.birdtricks.com/conure.htm>

United Kingdom Websites:

"Conure Training." Parrot-Link.co.uk. <http://www.parrot-link.co.uk/topic/25915-conure-training>

"Clicker Training." ProblemParrots.co.uk. <http://www.problemparrots.co.uk/clicker-training>

"How to Stop Your Conure from Screaming." BirdTrader.co.uk. <http://www.birdtrader.co.uk/bird_advice/how-to-stop-your-conure-from-screaming/423>

Index

Photo Credits

Title Page Photo By Flick user Takashi (aes256),
<http://www.flickr.com/photos/htakashi/6838387723/sizes/z
/in/photostream/>

Page 1 Photo By Eric Sonstroem from California, USA
(Green-Cheeked Conure Uploaded by snowmanradio)
[CC-BY-2.0 (http://creativecommons.org/licenses/by/2.0)],
via Wikimedia Commons,
<http://commons.wikimedia.org/wiki/File:Pyrrhura_molina
e_-pet-8a.jpg>

Page 3 Photo By turtlemom4bacon from Orlando, FL, USA
[CC-BY-SA-2.0 (http://creativecommons.org/licenses/by-
sa/2.0)], via Wikimedia Commons,
<http://commons.wikimedia.org/wiki/File:Aratinga_solstitia
lis_-pet_on_shoulder-8a.jpg>

Page 8 Photo 1By therouxdown (Riley Uploaded by
Snowmanradio) [CC-BY-SA-2.0
(http://creativecommons.org/licenses/by-sa/2.0)], via
Wikimedia Commons,
<http://commons.wikimedia.org/wiki/File:Pyrrhura_molina
e_-pineapple_mutation_-50_days_old-6b.jpg>

Page 10 Photo By Jnubbca (Own work) [GFDL
(http://www.gnu.org/copyleft/fdl.html) or CC-BY-SA-3.0
(http://creativecommons.org/licenses/by-sa/3.0)], via
Wikimedia Commons,
<http://commons.wikimedia.org/wiki/File:Stan_the_Sun_Co
nure.jpg>

<http://commons.wikimedia.org/wiki/File:Pyrrhura_molinae_-captive-perch-8a-1cp.jpg>

Page 100 Photo By Hans Hillewaert (Own work) [CC-BY-SA-3.0 (http://creativecommons.org/licenses/by-sa/3.0)], via Wikimedia Commons,
<http://commons.wikimedia.org/wiki/File:Aratinga_solstitialis_(trio).jpg>

References

"All About Conures." Nikki Moustaki.
<http://betterwords.typepad.com/birdvice/2009/01/conures-all-about-conures.html>

"Aratinga solstitialis." IUCN Red List.
<http://www.iucnredlist.org/details/106001572/0>

Berg, Linda. "Can Dogs and Birds Get Along?" Birds N
Ways. <http://www.birdsnways.com/wisdom/ww9e.htm>

"Bird Cage Selection Guide." Drs. Foster and Smith.
<http://www.drsfostersmith.com/pic/article.cfm?dept_id=&aid=110>

"Bird Medical Conditions." BirdChannel.com.
<http://www.birdchannel.com/diagnostics/default.aspx>

"Bird Nutrition: Feeding Pet Birds, Parrot Diets and
Nutrition Recommendations." PetEducation.com.
<http://www.peteducation.com/article.cfm?c=15+1835&aid=2844>

"Bird Safety: Bird Proof Your Home to Eliminate
Household Hazards." PetEducation.com.

<http://www.peteducation.com/article.cfm?c=15+1912&aid=3110>

"Birds You Don't Need a License to Keep." NSW Government – Environment & Heritage. <http://www.environment.nsw.gov.au/wildlifelicences/BirdsYouDontNeedALicenceToKeep.htm>

"Breeds and their Needs – Conures." Lakeland Bird Keepers. <http://www.lakelandbirdkeepers.co.uk/photogallery/breeds_their_needs_Conures.htm>

"Bringing Pet Birds into the UK." JCS Livestock. <http://www.jamescargo.com/livestock_transport/PetBirdImport.htm>

"Conures: Sun Conure." BirdTrader.co.uk. <http://www.birdtrader.co.uk/breed/conures-sun-conure/59>

"Conure Care." Animal-World Encyclopedia. <http://animal-world.com/encyclo/birds/conures/ConuresProfile.htm>

"FAQ: Feeding Green Cheeks." The Green Cheek Conure Home Page. <http://gcch.tripod.com/faq/faq6.html>

"Green Cheek Conure Diet." PawNation. <http://animals.pawnation.com/green-cheek-conure-diet>

"Green-Cheeked Conure." World Parrot Trust. <http://www.parrots.org/index.php/encyclopedia/captivestatus/green_cheeked_conure/>

"Green-Cheeked Conure Birds." BirdChannel.com. <http://www.birdchannel.com/bird-species>

"Green-Cheeked Conure Breeding/Reproduction." AvianWeb.com. <http://www.avianweb.com/greencheekedconurebreeding.html>

"How to Breed Conures: Breeding Sun Conures." Stuff4Petz.com. <http://stuff4petz.com/breeding>

"How to Convert Your Parrot to a Pellet Diet." BirdTrader.co.uk. <http://www.birdtrader.co.uk/bird_advice/how-to-convert-your-parrot-to-a-pellet-diet>

"How to Stop Your Conure from Screaming." BirdTrader.co.uk.

<http://www.birdtrader.co.uk/bird_advice/how-to-stop-your-conure-from-screaming/423>

"How to Treat and Prevent Conure Bleeding Syndrome." BirdTrader.co.uk.
<http://www.birdtrader.co.uk/bird_advice/how-to-treat-and-prevent-the-conure-bleeding-syndr/490>

"How to Trim a Conure's Feathers." BirdTrader.co.uk.
<http://www.birdtrader.co.uk/bird_advice/how-to-trim-a-conure-s-feathers/395>

"Leg Banding." AvianWeb.com.
<http://www.avianweb.com/legbands.html>

"Nutrition in Psittacines." Merck Veterinary Manual.
<http://www.merckmanuals.com/vet>

"Parrot Behavior Problems." FeatherMe.com.
<http://www.featherme.com/index.php/parrots-101/parrot-behavior>

"Polyomavirus Vaccination for Birds." Avian and Exotic Animal Care.
<http://avianandexotic.com/birds/polymarvirus-vaccination-for-birds>

"Proventricular Dilation Disease (PDD) or Macaw Wasting Disease." BirdTrader.co.uk. <http://www.birdtrader.co.uk/bird_advice/proventricular-dilatation-disease-pdd-or-macaw-was/515>

"Pyrrhura molinae." IUCN Red List. <http://www.iucnredlist.org/details/106001593/0>

"Raising Conures: Breeding and Raising Baby Sun Conures." Stuff4Petz.com. <http://stuff4petz.com/breeding>

"State Regulations & Restrictions on Caged Birds." International Parrot Society. <http://www.internationalparrotletsociety.org/stateimportregs.html>

Wilson, Liz. "Managing Parrot Behavior." Canadian Parrot Symposium. <http://www.silvio-co.com/cps/articles/1999/1999lwilson1.htm>

Made in the USA
Columbia, SC
05 April 2018